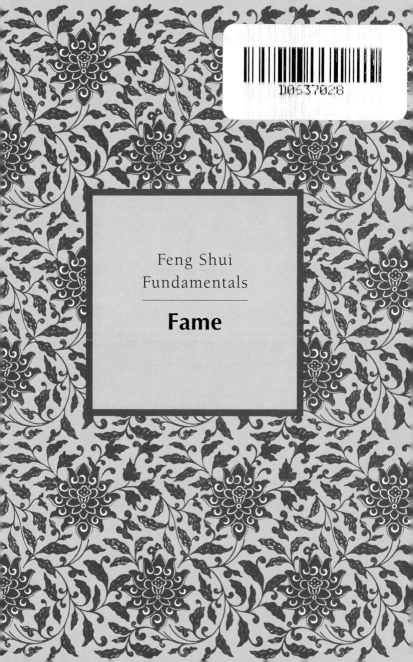

Feng Shui
Fundamentals

Fame

I dedicate this book with love, respect, and devotion to **Lama Zopa Rinpoche** my dearest kind lama.

To **Jennifer Too** my darling daughter, and in accordance with Rinpoche's request, to the ultimate happiness of all sentient beings of the world.

To the star waiting in the wings,
with love from Faye ×♡×

Feng Shui
Fundamentals

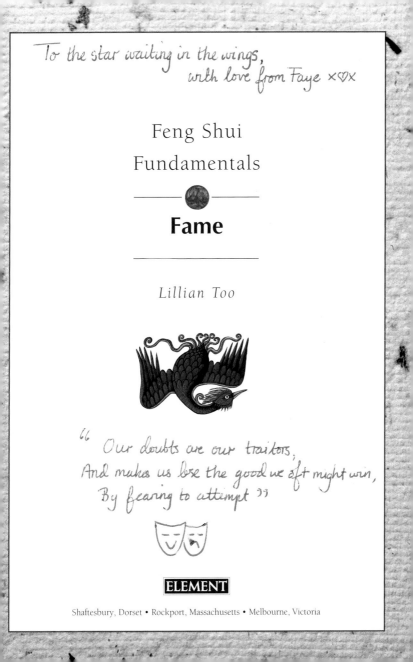

Fame

Lillian Too

" Our doubts are our traitors,
And makes us lose the good we oft might win,
By fearing to attempt "

ELEMENT

Shaftesbury, Dorset • Rockport, Massachusetts • Melbourne, Victoria

© Element Books Limited 1997
Text © Lillian Too 1997

First published in Great Britain by
ELEMENT BOOKS LIMITED
Shaftesbury, Dorset SP7 8BP

Published in the USA in 1997 by
ELEMENT BOOKS INC.
PO Box 830, Rockport, MA 01966

Published in Australia in 1997 by
ELEMENT BOOKS LIMITED
and distributed by Penguin Australia Ltd
487 Maroondah Highway, Ringwood, Victoria 3134

Designed and created with
THE BRIDGEWATER BOOK COMPANY LIMITED

ELEMENT BOOKS LIMITED
Editorial Director Julia McCutchen
Managing Editor Caro Ness
Production Director Roger Lane
Production Sarah Golden

THE BRIDGEWATER BOOK COMPANY LIMITED
Art Director Terry Jeavons
Designer James Lawrence
Managing Editor Anne Townley
Project Editor Andrew Kirk
Editor Linda Doeser
Picture Research Julia Hanson
Studio Photography Guy Ryecart
Illustrations Isabel Rayner, Andrew Kulman, Mark Jamieson,
Michaela Blunden, Paul Collicutt, Olivia Rayner, Jackie Harland

Printed and bound in Hong Kong

British Library Cataloguing in Publication Data available

Library of Congress Cataloging in Publication data available

ISBN 1 86204 121 0

The publishers wish to thank the following for the use of pictures:
Bridgeman Art Library, p 7; Elizabeth Whiting Associates, pp 20, 35.41; e.t. archive.p 12;
Julia Hanson, p 43; Image Bank, pp 8/9, 31; Rex, pp 9, 18;
and Zefa, pp 11, 17, 19, 23, 34, 35, 36, 44.

Special thanks go to:
Bright Ideas, Lewes, East Sussex
for help with properties

Lillian Too's website addresses are
http://www.asiaconnect.com.my/lillian-too
http://www.dragonmagic.com

Lillian Too's email addresses are
ltoo@dragonmagic.com
ltoo@popmail.asiaconnect.com.my

CONTENTS

INTRODUCTION TO FENG SHUI

WHAT IS FENG SHUI?

風水

Feng shui is the ancient Chinese science of arranging your personal surroundings and space so that the artificial structures we live in harmonize in an auspicious fashion with the intrinsic energies that swirl around the atmosphere. Feng shui can be as exacting as any mathematical system that involves precise calculations and measurements. However, it is also an art that requires subjective judgment, intuition, and careful interpretation.

The practice of feng shui incorporates the fundamental concepts of the Chinese view of the universe, and demands an understanding of these concepts, such as the need for balancing yin and yang forces and for harmonizing the combinations of the five elements.

Feng shui is an old science that has come down the centuries by word of mouth. This has turned much of the practice into superstition, and so not surprisingly there are several different approaches. Differences in dialect alone account for many of the variations of modern interpretation. Nevertheless, effective feng shui science is always based substantially on the surviving classical texts and the ancient symbols that make up its core. The two most important symbols are the eight-sided Pa Kua and the nine-sector grid – the Lo Shu square.

In the past, feng shui practice was mainly confined to the upper classes of China, so that the secret formulas of feng shui were always carefully guarded. Increasingly, however, these formulas, which unlock the mysteries of the Pa Kua's cryptic markings and the Lo Shu square's special arrangement of numbers, are being released by practitioners, thereby putting feng shui within reach of anyone and everyone.

The covenants of feng shui are exciting because they offer the attainment of almost every human aspiration. The system offers various methods and guidelines on how homes should be oriented, doors positioned, rooms arranged, furniture placed, and objects displayed – to tap into the beneficial energies that cause intangible forces to generate good fortune.

Feng shui holds out the promise of every kind of good fortune – wealth, health, prosperity, career success, a happy marriage, a good family life, respected descendants, the help of powerful people, and a life of recognition and repute. Based on the premise that the quality and attributes of the energies that flow around our living space affect our physical well-being, feng shui addresses all the ways people can manipulate these energies so that they are beneficial rather than harmful. Feng shui means "wind and water," and refers to the intangible forces that surround us. Thus the concept of energy is funda-mental to the practice of feng shui.

The Chinese call this energy sheng chi if it is beneficial, and shar chi if it is poisonous and deadly. In more lyrical language, sheng chi is also referred to as the dragon's cosmic breath, the dragon being a mythical celestial creature that is also the ultimate symbol of good fortune.

This book will show the reader how to achieve respect and recognition in their chosen field of endeavor. Practiced to the full, this aspect of feng shui promises the attainment of great fame and success, but even those who choose to remain anonymous or to maintain a low profile can use the methods explained in this book to gain the recognition that is such a vital and integral part of success.

Feng shui was originally confined to the upper classes in imperial China, and the formulas were a closely guarded secret.

~ 7 ~

THE CHINESE VIEW OF REPUTATION

For the Chinese, having a good name and reputation is one of the most important virtues. When you have a reputation for being honorable, honest, worthy, loyal, and possessing great integrity, then you are said to be a superior man. The list of positive attributes can be rather long and many Chinese classics that encompass all three of the major philosophies of China – Taoism, Confucianism, and Buddhism – go to great lengths to advocate and explain the need for living such a life. Individual good name and the good name of the family are most important. Without these, everything else becomes hollow and insubstantial.

Nowhere are the attributes of the superior man more eloquently described than in the I Ching, the Book of Changes, perhaps the greatest classic of Chinese thought to have survived the centuries. Both Taoism and Confucianism derive much of their philosophy from this great text. Feng shui also draws from its teachings and, indeed, much feng shui interpretation is guided by the meanings attributed to trigrams, the three-lined symbols that feature so prominently in feng shui analysis. These trigrams are the root symbols of the I Ching's 64 hexagram symbols.

There are many references to the superior man in the I Ching and the underlying assumption of the aspect of

feng shui covered in this book is the need to arrange our immediate environment in such a way that we live our lives according to the attributes of a superior man and, more significantly, that we are also recognized, respected, and looked up to as such. The feng shui in this book thus addresses the attainment of a good reputation. This involves tapping into the beneficial energies that bring recognition of our good qualities and abilities. Good

find it difficult to get themselves noticed, let alone respected and recognized. Without the luck of fame feng shui, success will be truly hard to come by.

No matter what attribute inspires respect and recognition, if you have a good and sound reputation, only then can success be attained. Thus everyone needs to tap into this aspect of luck, but the more your success is dependent on public and universal approval, the more you will need it.

Politicians, professionals, business leaders, managers, singers, models, doctors, lawyers – whatever your profession, the more you are recognized and respected as someone of substance, as a superior man, the more success you will have. Good feng shui helps you draw on the chi of the earth dragon for a little of this most valuable type of good luck.

fortune chi will help us get noticed, bring us the respect of our peers and colleagues and, ultimately, bring widespread fame and fortune to the determined and the talented.

Recognition is the underlying requirement of success. There are any number of people who work hard, who possess great talent and ability, yet who seem to

The hypothesis of the superior man is an abstraction central to the philosophies expounded in the I Ching. It has to do with perceived behavior, attributes, and attitudes. All references to the superior man apply also to the superior woman.

THE YIN AND YANG OF REPUTATIONS

The Chinese often refer to those perceived to be hugely successful as having a life that seems to be very yang. This has its roots in the belief that it is the yang energies of the self and the environment that propel men and women to attain heights of achievement and then to be recognized for them.

What is referred to is the energetic lively side of the yin yang cosmology. According to the Chinese view of the universe, all things are possessed of either yin or yang energies and it is the balanced complementarity of these two primordial and opposite energies that creates wholeness. Neither an excess of yin or of yang is regarded as being favorable or auspicious. There must always be a proper balance of these two forces, simply because one gives rise to the existence of the other. Thus, without yin, there cannot be yang and vice versa.

Yin energies describe the somber side. Yin is symbolized by darkness, the coldness of winter, the moon, stillness, and death. The colors of yin are dark or black – morose, forbidding, and also cool and lifeless.

Yang energies describe the brighter side of life. Yang is activity and noise, the

Yin is dark and quiet and, when there is balance, within the yin is a little bit of yang.

Yang is bright and lively and, for there to be balance, within the yang is a little bit of yin.

vibrancy and warmth of summer, the sun, and daytime. The colors of yang are bright and happy – white, sunshine yellow, and red. Of these colors, it is red that most eloquently symbolizes cheerful yang energies.

A basic tenet of feng shui is the requirement that yin and yang should always balance in a harmonious fashion. However, this does not mean there should be an equal amount of both within the environment. Their particular attributes must always be considered. Thus the houses of the living (as opposed to cemeteries and grave sites, the houses of the dead) are known as yang dwellings. There, yang energies are vital for life, but never to the extent that yin is totally overshadowed. When there is a total absence of yin, yang itself does not exist. This state is, of course, never possible, since yin energies come with the night and the changing of the seasons. An excess of yin energy is exceedingly harmful. In addition, because recognition and fame are strongly associated with yang energy, too much yin literally consumes all the yang luck needed.

Feng shui practitioners who want to activate the luck of recognition and reputation must focus significant attention on creating strong yang energy within the home, at the same time making sure that yin energy is never forgotten or overshadowed. The feng shui of fame and recognition requires an abundance of yang energy and this is achieved in a variety of ways, the most basic of which are to make clever use of the color red and to activate the fire element. Then focus on activating the corners of the home that represent fame and recognition luck.

The color red and the element of fire are most symbolic of yang. When correctly incorporated into the decor and design of home furnishings, red and the fire element can be powerful energizers.

THE MAIN TOOLS
OF FENG SHUI

THE FENG SHUI COMPASS

Known as the Luo Pan, this was the main reference tool used by feng shui master practitioners of another age. Indeed, many modern day feng shui consultants in Asia, especially in Hong Kong, Taiwan, Singapore, and Malaysia, still carry them as part of their working paraphernalia. For accuracy of readings,

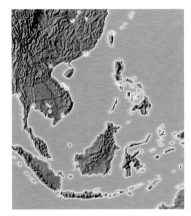

The Luo Pan has the compass in the center and around it are concentric rings of symbols and codes that represent the reference tools of the feng shui Master.

however, many also supplement the old-school compasses with modern Western-style compasses.

The Luo Pan has a compass in the center, with the needle pointing south. This is in keeping with the Chinese tradition of placing south at the top. However, in practice, this south is exactly the same as that indicated by any Western compass. The north of feng shui is also the same magnetic north referred to in western compass terminology. The first set of compass directions divides space into eight directions, consisting of the four cardinal directions – north, south, east, and west – and the four secondary directions – southwest, southeast, northwest, and northeast.

Immediately adjacent to the compass are the relevant matching trigrams. There are a total of eight and they are arranged round the Luo Pan according to the way they are placed around the Pa Kua (see page 14). These trigrams offer powerful meanings to the directions and form much of the fundamental basis of feng shui practice.

Then there are the sub-directions of the eight main directions. In all, the Luo Pan divides space into 24 sub-categories. Thus there are three sub-directions for every main direction. For example, south has three sub-categories of south. This is because many of the advanced formulas of

feng shui require extreme accuracy when taking directions, since their potency depends entirely on it.

There then follows element notations and further concentric rings of other codes and symbols. The more advanced the feng shui practice, the larger the number of rings.

In practical feng shui, the Luo Pan compass can be applied to a room, house, apartment, entire building, a complex of buildings, a city, and even a country. The exact codes often differ according to which Master's feng shui method is being applied and old Masters often have their own codes and notes written on their personal Luo Pans, which are therefore carefully guarded.

For the layman practitioner, a Western boy scout compass is usually good enough and, indeed, is preferable for convenience as well as accuracy.

For amateur practitioners, the deep meanings of the Luo Pan are not necessary. It is sufficient to use a compass to identify directions to obtain your orientation and to understand the relationship between trigrams, elements, and directions. This simplifies the practice tremendously, but this simplicity of approach is nevertheless just as potent.

THE PA KUA

The feng shui compass derives much of its meanings from the eight-sided Pa Kua symbol. Each of the sides represents one of the eight directions of the compass and, in accordance with Chinese tradition, the direction south is placed at the top. This is significant since the meanings and attributes of all the directions are determined from the eight trigrams placed round the Pa Kua. It is important in feng shui that the correct correlation between directions and trigrams are made. From here we can then proceed to another stage, which involves the five elements.

Practical feng shui involves studying directions, trigrams, and elements – and then interpreting the relationships between these three important reference tools. It is very easy to study and understand how to apply them in a practical manner. This is a fundamental approach and, once it has been mastered, it becomes increasingly easy to go deeper, at every stage peeling further layers of meanings from the Pa Kua.

There are two arrangements of the trigrams around the Pa Kua: The Early Heaven Arrangement and the Later Heaven Arrangement.

The Pa Kua shown here is that of the Later Heaven Arrangement, which is always the one used when diagnosing the feng shui of yang dwellings.

Under this arrangement, the trigram that represents brightness, fire, and widespread fame and recognition – Li – is placed in the south. This is therefore the most significant direction for those who wish to activate their reputation luck.

THE LO SHU SQUARE

A second vitally important tool of feng shui is the Lo Shu square. This is a nine-sector grid, each sector of which contains a number from one to nine The numbers are arranged in the grid so that the sum of any three, horizontally, vertically, or diagonally, is 15, the number of days it takes the moon to grow from new to full moon. The Chinese believe that this is a magic square and that it provides the key to unlocking many of the secrets of the Pa Kua.

The amateur practitioner should be familiar with the Lo Shu and its arrangement of numbers. Thus, since we have identified the south as the important direction to activate to achieve reputation luck, we can now take note that when we superimpose the Lo Shu onto the Pa Kua, the number that corresponds to the direction south is nine. By itself, nine is also believed to be an extraordinarily auspicious number, representing the fullness of heaven and earth. Correctly energizing this number is one of the methods that can be used to attract the good fortune we desire.

It is believed that the Lo Shu square appeared several thousand years ago on the back of a turtle that emerged from the River Lo. The Lo Shu square features prominently in feng shui technology, particularly in some of the more advanced formulas.

ENERGIZING THE PA KUA

Activating reputation and fame luck starts with understanding the Pa Kua. By itself, the Pa Kua (of the Early Heaven Arrangement) is believed to be a powerful protective tool and merely hanging it above the main door outside the home is deemed very effective in countering any negative energies that may be threatening the home and its residents. However, the Pa Kua, with its aggregated circles of meaning, is also a feng shui reference tool. We have seen that there is meaning in each of the trigrams placed at each of its edges.

Trigrams are three-lined symbols. These lines may be solid, yang lines or broken, yin lines. The relationship between the yin and yang lines is what gives meanings to the trigrams, according to the ancient text called the I Ching, the Book of Changes.

THE DIRECTION SOUTH

The trigram that represents fame, recognition, and reputation is Li and, according to the Later Heaven Arrangement, this is placed in the south. Thus the southern corner of any home or room represents recognition, reputation, and fame. If this corner has good feng shui, residents will have the excellent good fortune of attaining great heights of recognition and fame.

If this corner has poor feng shui, however, bad luck will prevail and the residents of the house will find it difficult to command any respect. People patronize or look down on them and, despite genuine efforts, recognition does not come. At its worst, bad feng shui in this corner could even lead to massive loss of face and severe damage to reputation and prestige, such as being convicted, becoming involved in a scandal, or simply being bad-mouthed by your enemies.

Reputation and fame feng shui requires you to make a careful examination of this sector of the room or home and, in particular, the meaning of the trigram Li.

LI

 This trigram is made up of one broken, yin line embraced by two unbroken, yang lines. It appears strong on the outside, yet is yielding and weak on the inside.

Li is the trigram that symbolizes the brightness of fire and the dazzle of the sun. It stands for glory and the applause of the masses. It also suggests activity and heat. The symbolism of this trigram is that of a great man who perpetuates the light by rising to prominence. His name and fame illuminate the four corners of the universe, dazzling one and all with his exemplary behavior and his magnificent talents and achievements.

At its ultimate, Li also represents lightning from which we can gauge the intrinsic brilliance of what it stands for. The color of Li is red, the bright and auspicious color that suggests celebrations and happy occasions. Li is the summer, and its energies are more yang than yin.

PRODUCTIVE CYCLE

This illustration shows the productive cycle of the five elements - earth, metal, water, wood, and fire. Wood, the element that produces fire, is in a positive position in relation to fire and is therefore helping to energize fire, which is associated with fame success.

APPLYING FIVE ELEMENT ANALYSIS

The best method of energizing the south, and thereby activating fame luck, is to apply the rationale of the five elements. According to the classical feng shui texts, all things in the universe, tangible or intangible, belong to one of five elements. These are fire, wood, water, metal, and earth. The elements combine with one another in different quantities to create all the permutations that are found in nature. They are said to interact with each other in never-ending productive and destructive cycles. Element analysis in feng shui requires an understanding of how the cycles work and how they may be applied in a practical way.

THE FIRE ELEMENT

The ruling element of the south is fire, symbolized by bright lights, the sun, the color red, and anything else that suggests fire. Identifying the relevant element to activate is a vital part of feng shui application. It suggests that placing, for instance, a fireplace in the south will activate excellent opportunities for becoming famous and widely respected. This particular type of luck is especially vital for politicians, models, singers, actors, and everyone engaged in professions that require them to be well known and easily recognized. In addition, from the cycles shown here, you will see several other attributes of the fire element.

- Fire is produced by wood, so wood is said to be good for it.
- Fire itself produces earth, so earth is said to exhaust it.
- Fire is destroyed by water, so water is said to be harmful to it.
- Fire destroys metal, so it is said to overcome metal.

From these attributes we know that to strengthen the element of the south we can use objects that symbolize both the fire and the wood elements, but that we should strenuously avoid anything belonging to the water element. This means that the south may be activated by any object, color, or painting that suggests wood or fire. Wooden paneling on the south wall or a display of dried driftwood, for example, would both be auspicious – because wood creates fire. Bright lights would be excellent. Anything colored red would also be good.

It is important to understand that any water feature would be deadly. According to feng shui, there is small water and big water. While small water would be relatively harmless, big water could be extremely damaging. A small aquarium would probably cause little trouble, but it is better to place it somewhere else. A swimming pool in the south corner of the garden or a large water painting above the fireplace in the south part of the living room, however, would be very harmful indeed. They could precipitate a scandal or bring shame and downfall to the breadwinner of the family. It would be prudent to be careful.

DESTRUCTIVE CYCLE

This illustration shows the destructive cycle of the five elements. Fire is being overwhelmed by water, the element that destroys fire. This means that fire, which is associated with fame luck, is not being strengthened.

ENERGIZING THE FIRE ELEMENT

In feng shui, each of the five elements is activated when objects that belong to the element group are present. To energize the fire element of the south, the fame corner, one of the best and easiest methods is to use bright lights – spotlights, crystal chandeliers, twinkling lights. Lights also signify valuable yang energy and so they are especially potent. Indeed, even if fame luck is not necessarily what you particularly want to achieve, installing a bright light and keeping it turned on for at least three hours each evening is always good feng shui.

Lights can be installed in many different ways. Hung from the ceiling, installed as wall brackets, placed on table tops as lamps, or concealed at floor level and shining upward – all these methods are acceptable. In fact, every kind of lighting is acceptable. You can let your own ideas and creativity flow. The lights can be very bright or subdued. The only taboos are that they should be white, yellow, or red, not blue or any of the other yin colors, and that you should refrain from using lampshades or table lamps shaped in a way that creates hostile vibes because they have sharp points or resemble a threatening object. Many modern table lamps have shapes that send out negative energies that are strengthened because of the light itself.

LIGHTING

This table lamp is an excellent feng shui energizer. Its round shape and colors are auspicious.

Spotlights can be very effective when shining directly at the south wall of a room. Just be careful that residents do not suffer from the glare. This will represent an excess of yang energy, which is not advisable.

CRYSTAL CHANDELIERS

If you can afford them, crystal chandeliers make excellent feng shui energizers. The facets of the crystal greatly enhance the light and, if kept switched on, crystal chandeliers in the south corner of any room really do bring auspicious luck to residents.

CRYSTALS

If you cannot afford a chandelier, look for small, faceted crystal balls and hang them with a red thread near a light or in front of windows bathed with sunshine. This brings valuable yang energies into the home, sometimes causing the sunlight to break up into colorful rainbows that are reflected on walls and ceilings.

Table lamps like this one are not very effective for energizing the fire element because the shape is not friendly.

THE COLOR RED

The color red is particularly meaningful for activating the recognition factor to maximize success. It is the universally accepted color of good fortune and always present during important festivals and celebrations. Chinese brides almost always wear red, and the birth of a son is celebrated with eggs dyed red. The lunar new year is celebrated by wearing red and the gift of red packets of lucky money to children and employees.

It follows that in feng shui, the color red is also very significant, especially when energizing the south corner of the home to encourage good fortune chi to be created there. It is, therefore, most important to incorporate this most auspicious color in furnishings and decorations if residents wish to benefit from good reputation luck.

Eggs dyed red are used by the Chinese to celebrate the birth of a son.

Red packets are presented to children and employees to celebrate New Year.

Many everyday objects with red as their dominant color can be displayed in the south. These include soft furnishings, such as upholstery, lampshades, drapes, bed spreads, rugs, and carpets.

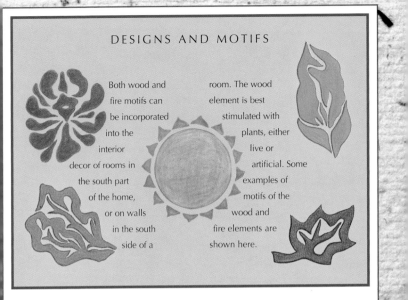

DESIGNS AND MOTIFS

Both wood and fire motifs can be incorporated into the interior decor of rooms in the south part of the home, or on walls in the south side of a room. The wood element is best stimulated with plants, either live or artificial. Some examples of motifs of the wood and fire elements are shown here.

USING OBJECTS OF THE FIRE ELEMENT

The fireplace is, perhaps, one of the most effective ways of energizing the fire element of the south. This is especially significant during winter months when a great deal of yin energy is present, reflected in the cold weather and the long nights. It is during this season that the bright, warm, lively, and cheering yang energy of the fireplace is most needed.

Placing a painting with red as the dominant color or a photograph frame made of wood (since wood produces fire) above the fireplace would be excellent supplements to the fire element.

The warmth of this fire on the south wall restores weak yang energy perfectly.

INDIVIDUAL FAME
SUCCESS ORIENTATIONS

THE COMPASS FORMULA

名聲

Your fame success direction, based on your date of birth, can be calculated using a potent compass feng shui formula that for many years was a closely guarded secret. It is derived from the two principal symbols of feng shui – the eight-sided Pa Kua, with its layers of meaning, and the Lo Shu magic square, a nine-sector grid that further unlocks the secrets of the ancient Pa Kua.

Also known as the Pa Kua Lo Shu formula (Kua formula for short), this method of investigating personal success orientations was given to the author's feng shui Master by an old Taiwan feng shui Grand Master who was a legend in his time. As the personal consultant of many of Taiwan's most prominent men of an earlier era, Master Chan Chuan Huay was an expert on feng shui that would bring success, wealth, and power. He was in possession of this Kua formula and used it with great success for his clients, many of whom founded huge business conglomerates and

rose to positions of authority and power. It is no coincidence that the small island of Taiwan is so successful; feng shui has always been widely practiced there.

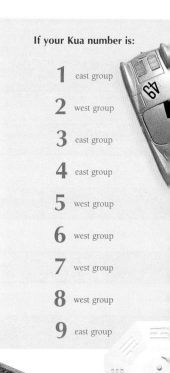

If your Kua number is:

1 east group

2 west group

3 east group

4 east group

5 west group

6 west group

7 west group

8 west group

9 east group

THE KUA FORMULA

To determine your success orientation, first determine your Kua number. Obtain your Chinese year of birth, based on the calendar on pages 28–29 and use the following calculation to get your Kua number. Remember that there is no Kua number 5 – males with Kua number 5 should use 2, females should use 8. For clarity, Kua number 5 is shown below.

THE KUA FORMULA

Calculate your Kua number as follows. Add the last two digits of your Chinese year of birth. e.g. **1965**, **6+5=11**. If the sum is higher than ten, reduce to a single digit, thus **1+1=2**.

Males	Females
Subtract from	Add
10	**5**
thus	thus
10-2	**5+2**
=8	**=7**
So, for men born in	So, for women born in
1965	**1965**
the Kua number is	the Kua number is
8	**7**

Now check against this table for your family direction and location.

Your Fame and Success orientation is:

SOUTHEAST for both males and females

NORTHEAST for both males and females

SOUTH for both males and females

NORTH for both males and females

NORTHEAST for males and
SOUTHWEST for females

WEST for both males and females

NORTHWEST for both males and females

SOUTHWEST for both males and females

EAST for both males and females

THE CHINESE CALENDAR

Note that for the Chinese the New Year begins in either late January or early February. When calculating your Kua number, do take note of this. Thus if you are born in January 1946 before the New Year, your Chinese year of birth is said to be 1945 and not 1946. This calendar also indicates the ruling element of your year of birth. This gives you further clues on which corner of the home, based on your element, will have the most effect on your well-being.

Year	From	To	Element	Year	From	To	Element
1900	31 Jan 1900	18 Feb 1901	Metal	1923	16 Feb 1923	4 Feb 1924	Water
1901	19 Feb 1901	17 Feb 1902	Metal	1924	5 Feb 1924	24 Jan 1925	Wood
1902	18 Feb 1902	28 Jan 1903	Water	1925	25 Jan 1925	12 Feb 1926	Wood
1903	29 Jan 1903	15 Jan 1904	Water	1926	13 Feb 1926	1 Feb 1927	Fire
1904	16 Feb 1904	3 Feb 1905	Wood	1927	2 Feb 1927	22 Jan 1928	Fire
1905	4 Feb 1905	24 Jan 1906	Wood	1928	23 Jan 1928	9 Feb 1929	Earth
1906	25 Jan 1906	12 Feb 1907	Fire	1929	10 Feb 1929	29 Jan 1930	Earth
1907	13 Feb 1907	1 Feb 1908	Fire	1930	30 Jan 1930	16 Feb 1931	Metal
1908	2 Feb 1908	21 Jan 1909	Earth	1931	17 Feb 1931	15 Feb 1932	Metal
1909	22 Jan 1909	9 Feb 1910	Earth	1932	16 Feb 1932	25 Jan 1933	Water
1910	10 Feb 1910	29 Jan 1911	Metal	1933	26 Jan 1933	13 Feb 1934	Water
1911	30 Jan 1911	17 Feb 1912	Metal	1934	14 Feb 1934	3 Feb 1935	Wood
1912	18 Feb 1912	25 Feb 1913	Water	1935	4 Feb 1935	23 Jan 1936	Wood
1913	26 Feb 1913	25 Jan 1914	Water	1936	24 Jan 1936	10 Feb 1937	Fire
1914	26 Jan 1914	13 Feb 1915	Wood	1937	11 Feb 1937	30 Jan 1938	Fire
1915	14 Feb 1915	2 Feb 1916	Wood	1938	31 Jan 1938	18 Feb 1939	Earth
1916	3 Feb 1916	22 Jan 1917	Fire	1939	19 Feb 1939	7 Feb 1940	Earth
1917	23 Jan 1917	10 Feb 1918	Fire	1940	8 Feb 1940	26 Jan 1941	Metal
1918	11 Feb 1918	31 Jan 1919	Earth	1941	27 Jan 1941	14 Feb 1942	Metal
1919	1 Feb 1919	19 Feb 1920	Earth	1942	15 Feb 1942	24 Feb 1943	Water
1920	20 Feb 1920	7 Feb 1921	Metal	1943	25 Feb 1943	24 Jan 1944	Water
1921	8 Feb 1921	27 Jan 1922	Metal	1944	25 Jan 1944	12 Feb 1945	Wood
1922	28 Jan 1922	15 Feb 1923	Water	1945	13 Feb 1945	1 Feb 1946	Wood

Year	From	To	Element	Year	From	To	Element
1946	2 Feb 1946	21 Jan 1947	Fire	1977	18 Feb 1977	6 Feb 1978	Fire
1947	22 Jan 1947	9 Feb 1948	Fire	1978	7 Feb 1978	27 Jan 1979	Earth
1948	10 Feb 1948	28 Jan 1949	Earth	1979	28 Jan 1979	15 Feb 1980	Earth
1949	29 Jan 1949	16 Feb 1950	Earth	1980	16 Feb 1980	4 Feb 1981	Metal
1950	17 Feb 1950	5 Feb 1951	Metal	1981	5 Feb 1981	24 Jan 1982	Metal
1951	6 Feb 1951	26 Jan 1952	Metal	1982	25 Jan 1982	12 Feb 1983	Water
1952	27 Jan 1952	13 Feb 1953	Water	1983	13 Feb 1983	1 Feb 1984	Water
1953	14 Feb 1953	2 Feb 1954	Water	1984	2 Feb 1984	19 Feb 1985	Wood
1954	3 Feb 1954	23 Jan 1955	Wood	1985	20 Feb 1985	8 Feb 1986	Wood
1955	24 Jan 1955	11 Feb 1956	Wood	1986	9 Feb 1986	28 Jan 1987	Fire
1956	12 Feb 1956	30 Jan 1957	Fire	1987	29 Jan 1987	16 Feb 1988	Fire
1957	31 Jan 1957	17 Feb 1958	Fire	1988	17 Feb 1988	5 Feb 1989	Earth
1958	18 Feb 1958	7 Feb 1959	Earth	1989	6 Feb 1989	26 Jan 1990	Earth
1959	8 Feb 1959	27 Jan 1960	Earth	1990	27 Jan 1990	14 Feb 1991	Metal
1960	28 Jan 1960	14 Feb 1961	Metal	1991	15 Feb 1991	3 Feb 1992	Metal
1961	15 Feb 1961	4 Feb 1962	Metal	1992	4 Feb 1992	22 Jan 1993	Water
1962	5 Feb 1962	24 Jan 1963	Water	1993	23 Jan 1993	9 Feb 1994	Water
1963	25 Jan 1963	12 Feb 1964	Water	1994	10 Feb 1994	30 Jan 1995	Wood
1964	13 Feb 1964	1 Feb 1965	Wood	1995	31 Jan 1995	18 Feb 1996	Wood
1965	2 Feb 1965	20 Jan 1966	Wood	1996	19 Feb 1996	7 Feb 1997	Fire
1966	21 Jan 1966	8 Feb 1967	Fire	1997	8 Feb 1997	27 Jan 1998	Fire
1967	9 Feb 1967	29 Jan 1968	Fire	1998	28 Jan 1998	15 Feb 1999	Earth
1968	30 Jan 1968	16 Feb 1969	Earth	1999	16 Feb 1999	4 Feb 2000	Earth
1969	17 Feb 1969	5 Feb 1970	Earth	2000	5 Feb 2000	23 Jan 2001	Metal
1970	6 Feb 1970	26 Jan 1971	Metal	2001	24 Jan 2001	11 Feb 2002	Metal
1971	27 Jan 1971	15 Feb 1972	Metal	2002	12 Feb 2002	31 Jan 2003	Water
1972	16 Feb 1972	22 Feb 1973	Water	2003	1 Feb 2003	21 Jan 2004	Water
1973	23 Feb 1973	22 Jan 1974	Water	2004	22 Jan 2004	8 Feb 2005	Wood
1974	23 Jan 1974	10 Feb 1975	Wood	2005	9 Feb 2005	28 Jan 2006	Wood
1975	11 Feb 1975	30 Jan 1976	Wood	2006	29 Jan 2006	17 Feb 2007	Fire
1976	31 Jan 1976	17 Feb 1977	Fire	2007	18 Feb 2007	6 Feb 2008	Fire

APPLYING THE KUA FORMULA

Once you know your fame and success direction, there are several ways you can match your own energy with that of your surroundings, thus activating success chi to your advantage.

Your Kua number gives you the most auspicious direction to activate for this purpose. It also identifies your luckiest compass location and your luckiest Lo Shu number. The luck referred to here is money and success luck, as well as fame, recognition, and respect. When you activate this personal success direction and location, you greatly enhance your chances of attaining success in your chosen field of endeavor.

HOW TO DO IT

The home layout should be demarcated into the nine equal sectors according to the Lo Shu grid as shown. To do this accurately, use a good compass (any Western compass will do) and a good measuring tape. Then, standing in the center of the home, identify the locations and divide the total floor space of the home into nine equal grids. This is shown in the diagram here.

Superimpose the nine-sector grid onto your home layout plan and then use it to identify the location that is most auspicious for you. Try to locate your main door, your study, or bedroom here.

N

Nine equal grids.

THE MAIN DOOR

If your main door is placed in your success location and is facing your success direction, your home luck will be maximized. If for instance, your success direction is north, as shown here, then that is where your main door should be located and should face.

IRREGULAR-SHAPED HOMES

Houses and apartments rarely have regular, square, or rectangular shapes, making it difficult to superimpose a nine-sector grid onto the layout. More serious still is the problem of missing corners. There are ways of getting round this problem, but what you do depends on your circumstances and whether you have the available space. Some of the more common problems are shown here.

Installing a light is one solution to the problem of missing corners.

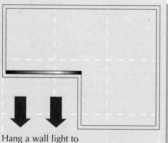

Hang a wall light to offset the problem of missing corners.

There are several possible solutions you can put in place:

- ▒ Install a light.
- ▒ Hang a wall mirror.
- ▒ Build an extension.

According to feng' shui, missing corners mean the home will be lacking in certain luck aspects. What type of luck is missing depends on the corresponding compass direction of the missing sector. If one missing sector represents your fame and reputation direction, you would be well advised to make alterations to your house according to the solution that suits you best.

An irregular-shaped layout sometimes makes it difficult to have the main door located or oriented in the most

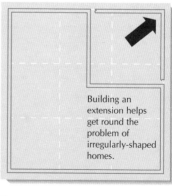

Building an extension helps get round the problem of irregularly-shaped homes.

auspicious way. If you cannot get the location you want, tapping the success direction alone is often good enough. If you cannot tap either the location or direction, try at least to have your main door face one of your four auspicious directions. Remember that directions are taken inside the home facing outward.

EAST AND WEST GROUP DIRECTIONS

Compass feng shui divides the human race into east and west groups, so your auspicious directions depend on whether you are an east or a west group person. This is based on your Kua number. East group people have Kua numbers one, three, four, and nine. East group directions are east, north, south, and southeast. West group people have Kua numbers two, five, six, seven, and eight. West group directions are west, southwest, northwest, and northeast. East group directions are extremely inauspicious for west group people and vice versa. Try at all costs to have your main entrance facing one of your group directions.

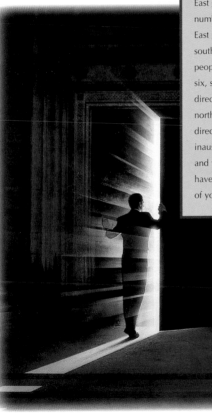

Try to position your main door to face your success direction so as to encourage good fame luck.

AVOIDING YOUR
TOTAL LOSS DIRECTION

When addressing the important matter of reputation, feng shui particularly warns against having a main door that faces one of your inauspicious directions, especially your chueh ming or total loss direction.

As the name implies, the total loss direction can be dangerous. People whose main door faces their chueh ming usually have more than their fair share of bad luck. None of their ventures seems to succeed, and opportunities slip by with annoying frequency. It is as if something blocks their luck. When their astrological period is bad, having such a main door orientation could even lead to scandal, as well as a major loss of reputation.

Determining your chueh ming direction depends on your Kua number. To safeguard yourself and your good name, you would be advised to check the table here and take counter-measures accordingly. The best way to correct this is to use another door as the main door. If this is not possible, re-orient your main door so that it faces at least one of your auspicious directions.

Your Kua number	Chueh Ming (Males)	Chueh Ming (Females)
1	SOUTH-WEST	SOUTH-WEST
2	NORTH	NORTH
3	WEST	WEST
4	NORTH-EAST	NORTH-EAST
5	NORTH	SOUTH-EAST
6	SOUTH	SOUTH
7	EAST	EAST
8	SOUTH-EAST	SOUTH-EAST
9	NORTH-WEST	NORTH-WEST

HOW TO RE-ORIENTATE YOUR MAIN DOOR

An east group door direction is changed to face northwest, a west group direction. Original door faces north. Door changed to face northwest.

Original door faces north.

New door is facing northwest.

The same east group door direction (facing north) is now changed to face northeast, a west group direction.

This house has another door that faces west. If north is your chueh ming direction, it would be better to use this second door as your main one.

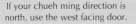

If your chueh ming direction is north, use the west facing door.

TIPS ABOUT MAIN DOORS

- A solid door is preferable to a glass door.
- A door should open inward and not outward.
- A conventional door is better than a sliding door.
- Let nothing block the outside or inside of the door.
- The door should be neither too big nor too small.
- Do not have two or three doors in a row.

PROTECTING THE MAIN DOOR

When activating your personalized success direction there are other significant feng shui guidelines that must be followed and incorporated into your plans. These have nothing to do with the formula itself, but combine the rules of form school feng shui with compass feng shui specifications.

In the practice of feng shui, basic form school principles must never be ignored. Indeed, you can have all the directions and orientations absolutely correct and yet be hit by what is termed killing breath or shar chi. This is so harmful that it negates all the good feng shui you may have carefully arranged. It is especially dangerous when your main

FROM THE OUTSIDE

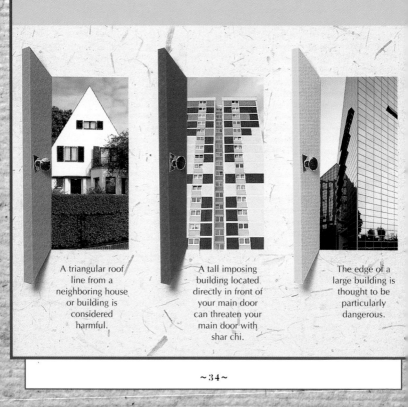

A triangular roof line from a neighboring house or building is considered harmful.

A tall imposing building located directly in front of your main door can threaten your main door with shar chi.

The edge of a large building is thought to be particularly dangerous.

entrance door is being hit directly by the killing breath. Shar chi is caused by threatening structures, known as poison arrows, that channel all the killing breath directly at your door.

THINGS TO WATCH OUT FOR

Structures that can hurt your main door are present in the immediate external environment and also inside the home itself. Some common examples are shown here. The golden rule is to be wary of anything that seems to block the good chi from coming in or seems to threaten the main door. With practice, once you live in a greater state of awareness of your surroundings, you will begin to spot these offending structures.

ON THE INSIDE

If the door opens directly on to a staircase, it is advisable to re-orient it, or you can simply turn the last step of the stairs to change the direction of the staircase.

If the door opens onto a toilet, the vibes are truly harmful. The toilet turns good luck chi into killing breath.

If the door directly faces a mirror, good luck chi that enters the home is absorbed. It is better to remove the mirror. If it faces a window, keep the window covered with drapes.

ACTIVATING THE PHOENIX

天獸

The feng huang or phoenix holds a very special place in Chinese traditional beliefs. In feng shui it represents the south and is one of the four celestial animals that symbolize classical landscape feng shui. When the crimson phoenix lies in front of the home, in view of the front door, it holds the promise of many wonderful opportunities for residents. Landscape and form school feng shui Masters interpret this to mean the presence of a small boulder or little hillock in front of the home to represent a comfortable footstool. Underlying this supportive role are all the other attributes of the phoenix. Because it presides over the south quadrant of the compass, the phoenix also symbolizes the sun and the warmth of summer – and a rich harvest.

This beautiful creature is believed to be the product of the fire as well as the sun, hence the famous saying – from the ashes, the phoenix rises. This is because fire produces earth (or ashes) in the cycle of the five elements. The phoenix is regarded as very yang, and is said to be wonderful for bringing outstanding fame luck, not only to the breadwinner, but also to the descendants of the household.

Hang a painting of the phoenix on the south wall, above the fireplace, against a red background. This creates auspicious fame luck. You should hang this picture in the living or family room rather than the bedroom or dining room.

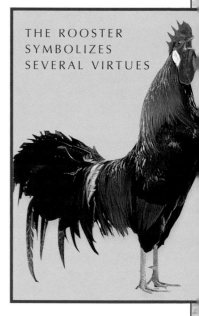

THE ROOSTER
SYMBOLIZES
SEVERAL VIRTUES

In Chinese art, the phoenix is adorned with stunningly beautiful plumage, as befits the king of feathered creatures. However, the phoenix is a legendary creature, and is said to appear only in times of peace and prosperity.

- The crown on his head is a mark of his literary skill and his passion for learning.
- The spurs on his feet represent his brave and courageous spirit.
- The rooster is an effective substitute for the phoenix because it is also regarded as the chief embodiment of the yang element, which represents the warmth and life of the universe.
- He crows without fail each morning to announce the dawn of a new day. He is thus faithful and reliable.

SUBSTITUTES

If you cannot find a painting of a phoenix, any earthenware with the phoenix painted on it can be a good substitute. If you really cannot find a phoenix, you can use a peacock or a rooster to symbolize the phoenix. Indeed, the Chinese believe all those born in a rooster year under the Chinese calendar have the potential to transform into the phoenix. This means that they achieve great fame and success and are highly respected and honored.

THE EIGHT ORDINARY SYMBOLS

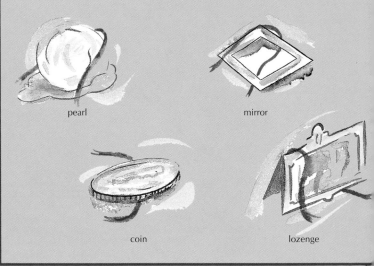

pearl

mirror

coin

lozenge

CLAIMING THE EIGHT TREASURES

To make the home auspicious, feng shui practitioners often claim the eight treasures by placing their symbols within the home and then activating their good qualities by tying them with red thread or placing them on a red tablecloth. There are several versions of these eight treasures and, unless one is well schooled in the classics and legends of ancient China, it is easy to become confused with the symbols. For feng shui purposes, it is sufficient to select the symbols from two versions.

The symbols are the dragon's pearl, the golden coin, the mirror, two books, the artemesia leaf, the stone chime, the rhinoceros' horns, and the lozenge. It is not necessary to use every one of them. The golden coin is a favorite "treasure" for using in this way since it also symbolizes wealth.

These good-luck symbols are believed to activate success luck within the home. Place one or all of them on a table in the living room in the corner that represents your success direction according to the Kua formula. Do not forget either to tie them with red thread or ribbon or to place a small piece of red cloth beneath them to activate their qualities.

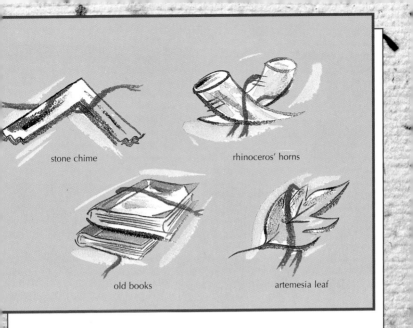

stone chime

rhinoceros' horns

old books

artemesia leaf

ACTIVATING THE COIN

Although you can use any coin to symbolize the good fortune of wealth, I always recommend using old Chinese coins which are round with a square hole in the center, symbolizing the unity of heaven and earth. In addition, the two sides of the coin symbolize yin and yang. The side with two characters is said to be the yin side, while the other with the four characters is said to be the yang side. For feng shui purposes, it is advisable to tie three of these old coins with a red thread and then place them, yang side up, in your auspicious corner. The coins can be hung, stuck onto the wall, or placed on the table top.

ACTIVATING THE DRAGON'S PEARL

The pearl is supposed to be the elusive essence of the moon goddess, and is said to act as a charm against too much fire. Thus it guards against the over-ambition that brings arrogance and the downfall of even the most powerful.

The pearl is also an emblem of genius, purity, and beauty. Generally, anything round or spherical can be said to represent the pearl. A ceramic model of the celestial dragon holding the pearl can be displayed on the dragon side of the home – the east – in order to attract good fortune luck to all the women of the family.

THE EIGHT AUSPICIOUS SYMBOLS

These eight symbols are believed to have appeared on the sole of the Buddha's foot. They are exceedingly popular among the Chinese who follow the Buddhist faith and are regarded with great respect. The eight symbols are the wheel, the conch shell, the umbrella, the canopy or flag, the lotus, the jar, the fish, and the mystic knot. These symbols can usually be seen in Chinese emporiums, particularly the fish, which is probably the most popular of the eight.

Legend tells us that images of the wheel, canopy, umbrella, fish, jar, conch shell, lotus, and mystic knot were revealed on Buddha's foot.

THE WHEEL

This is the symbol of a person whose conduct is honorable and upright. It represents authority and power achieved. It is sometimes replaced by the bell. Place it in your lucky direction and tie a red thread to activate it.

THE CANOPY

The canopy or flag is usually desorated with auspicious words or symbols and then hung in the breeze. It is believed that each time the breeze blows it activates the auspicious energy and good luck symbolized by the good fortune symbol placed on the flag. Usually canopies made of red-colored material are believed to bring good fortune.

THE UMBRELLA

This is an ancient emblem of dignity and high rank; in the old days, high officials were often presented with umbrellas to signify respect. This is also the emblem held by one of the four legendary kings, Mo Li Hung, the guardian of the south. Place an umbrella in the south corner of your home to signify protection from loss of name.

THE FISH

This is always symbolically applied as an emblem of wealth, mainly because phonetically the word fish in Chinese sounds like abundance. The sign of the double fish symbolizes happiness. Placing the symbol of the fish in the home signifies the successful attainment of one's goals.

THE LOTUS

This is one of the most popular emblems, signifying great achievements from the humblest beginnings, like a magnificent bloom rising out of muddy waters. The lotus is also symbolic of summer. Incorporate this motif into your soft furnishings if you wish to introduce this good-fortune symbol into your home.

THE JAR

A decorative jar, filled to the brim with water and placed near the entrance to the home is believed to symbolize great good fortune. Remember to keep the water fresh by changing it regularly, and keep a sense of balance by matching the size of the jar to the size of your home.

THE MYSTIC KNOT

This knot represents many things, including longevity, as it is endless, and love, because it has no beginning and no end.

The knot also represents the attainment of immortality for one's name. Feng shui Masters take their cue from the motifs seen in the palaces of the Forbidden City in Beijing and recommend the use of the knot to symbolize its attributes within the home.

THE CONCH SHELL

In the old days, this was a royal insignia, often used as a symbol to represent a prosperous voyage. It is supposed to attract excellent fame luck when mounted on a rosewood stand and displayed in the lucky corner of your home. In ancient times, the conch shell was also used as a trumpet, so it signifies your name being known far and wide.

The three star gods – Fuk, Luk and Sau – whose presence in the house is believed to offer symbolic protection of the family name.

WELCOMING THE THREE STAR GODS

Using feng shui to attract fame luck and protect the family name is a continuous process and much of this practice has, over the centuries, become part of annual traditional rituals observed during festive occasions, particularly the lunar New Year. This is always supposed to involve saying good-bye to the old year and welcoming in the new one.

Chinese homes start the process by displaying the three star gods – the God of Wealth, the God of Success, and the God of Longevity – prominently in the home to welcome their presence and their protection of the family's name, wealth, and health luck. This trinity of symbolic deities are known as the Fuk Luk Sau.

If you invite them into your home, place them in full view of the main door. These star gods are not worshipped, but displayed for their symbolic value. Nevertheless, they must be treated with respect and so should not be placed on the floor or lower than a table top.

KUAN KUNG

The figure of Kuan Kung, the patron saint of the Hong Kong police and the triads alike, is a powerful figure that represents divine protection. Kuan Kung was a general during the period of the three kingdoms and was deified by the Chinese. It is a good idea to display a figurine of any one of your military heroes to symbolize valor, courage, and bravery in the home.

The bat is almost always featured on the imperial robes of the emperor and his court, and on furniture. This is because it symbolizes longevity and extreme good fortune. In feng shui the bat is usually featured as a good-luck emblem, which it is recommended should be incorporated into the designs of soft furnishings.

LANTERNS AND FIRE CRACKERS

These are additional symbols of the fire element, which are used during festive occasions to activate vital yang energy for the household. Lanterns in various shapes and sizes symbolize fire in paper. Auspicious words are usually written on the lanterns to represent wealth or happiness. At the same time, fire crackers are let off to chase away any negative vibrations or naughty ghosts that may be tempted to cause trouble. The loud sound of crackers being fired is often heard during the lunar New Year. This symbolically ushers in a prosperous and auspicious New Year.

THE BAT

DRUMS, TRUMPETS, BELLS, AND WINDCHIMES

These symbols, which create sounds, are extremely useful for attracting the luck of fame and success into the home. Sounds also create yang energy. By themselves such symbols do not necessarily have the potency of the compass orientations. They are, however, excellent supplements to the Kua formula and the use of the eight treasures.

Drums and trumpets herald the coming of auspicious developments. If you have a musical family and these objects are present in your home, keep

The trumpet belongs to the metal element, and if played in the south part of the house, it will activate fame luck.

them in a room in the south part of the house or in the corner that represents your success direction. If possible, do your music practice in these rooms to help activate fame luck.

Bells and windchimes are objects that usually belong to the metal element and so are controlled by the fire element. Their sounds are very welcome in the south as well. They can be placed in the south part of the home or the south part of the family or living room. When using these objects to activate your personal success corner, however, it is necessary to be careful. Bells and windchimes should not be placed in the wood corners – east and southeast – because metal destroys wood. Therefore, if these happen to be your success directions, it is far better not to use these objects.

Drums create a lot of yang energy and herald auspicious events.

WINDCHIMES

These are also very useful for overcoming common feng shui problems encountered in any home. Hang them when a particularly threatening, exposed, overhead beam runs across your working desk, dining table, or living room. I am not keen on placing windchimes in the bedroom, since it is not advisable to activate too much yang energy there.

A windchime effectively deflects the bad feng shui of the overhead beam.

A windchime hung above the second door, when there are three doors in a row, deflects the bad feng shui of this feature,

HAZARDS AND HOW
TO COUNTER THEM

A toilet placed above the front door will fatally weaken the healthy chi which is coming into the house.

People who have their bedrooms below a toilet will find that unhealthy shar chi presses down on them causing sleeplessnes and ill-health

SOME COMMON FENG SHUI HAZARDS

A big part of feng shui practice is becoming accustomed to spotting arrangements or features within the home that can harm the family's finances and its good name. It is often easy to overlook this defensive aspect. In addition to protecting the main door, activating auspicious orientations, and energizing relevant corners within the home with good-fortune symbols, it is also useful to familiarize yourself with some common feng shui hazards that inadvertently destroy all the good feng shui so painstakingly put in. It is advisable to look out for these before embarking on a major feng shui improvement exercise.

LOCATION OF TOILETS

A very common cause of specific types of bad luck can often be traced to the location of certain rooms within the home. You have to be particularly careful about the toilet because it literally flushes away all the good luck represented by the corner in which it is located. Thus, if it is located in your marriage and love corner, your love life suffers, if it is located in your wealth corner, your money is flushed away, and if it is located in your success corner, you could well lose your money and experience a major setback in your career – your good name could become tarnished.

Make toilets within the home small and unobtrusive, so they constitute only a small part of any corner. If you have a large bath-cum-dressing area, screen off the toilet so that it is not easily visible. Toilets always create shar chi within the home and are best kept out of sight.

TOILETS

In the old days in China, palaces and wealthy homes had no toilets. Servants brought in tubs for bathing and toilets were carried in and out whenever needed. The poorer peasants who lived in the country also did not have toilets inside the home. They were always located some distance from the house itself.

NOTE

There were night soil carriers in ancient times, but the indoor toilet poses new problems. In addition to spoiling the luck of corners, toilets which are located above the main door (toilet on the upper floor) or toilets that share a wall with the master bed (in the next room) also bring bad luck. Be alert to these arrangements and arrange your main door and bed placement accordingly.

STOREROOMS AND KITCHENS

Storerooms are not as harmful as toilets, but when mops, brooms, and other cleaning paraphernalia are placed in storerooms in full view of the front door, they serve to chase away the good-fortune chi that enters the home. Keep your storerooms closed and your mops and brooms tidied away.

As a matter of fact, clutter is always frowned upon by feng shui Masters. There cannot be good balance when there are dirty clothes, stale food (very yin), and mess around. These are not conducive to attracting the good sheng chi to settle and accumulate.

Kitchen locations also suppress our good luck and it is important to make sure no exposed cooking and washing of dishes are done in the place that represents your personal success location, based on your Kua formula. Taking this feng shui warning into account, modern appliances, such as dishwashers, are an excellent way of overcoming this problem.

FIRE AT HEAVEN'S GATE.

A major feature to look out for in the kitchen is to ensure that a gas cooker is not placed in the northwest. If it is, you will be doing exposed cooking in the corner that is associated with the breadwinner or head of the household. The northwest is said to be the gate of heaven, since the matching trigram of this corner is Chien, representing heaven. Using fire to cook here is therefore like setting fire to heaven and burning the good fortune of the head of the household. Thus a naked flame in the northwest corner of your kitchen represents a destructive force rather than positive yang energy. You

Gas cookers involve exposed cooking – flames are created. If your cooker is in the northwest, move it to another location within the kitchen.

▦ The kitchen should never be located in the center of the home. This severely oppresses the family's luck, especially that of the head of the household – the breadwinner.

▦ A toilet should not directly face a kitchen, nor should there be one above the kitchen.

▦ The level of the kitchen should not be higher or lower than the dining area, but the same. It should definitely not be lower than the living area.

▦ The kitchen must not be round and should not be irregular-shaped. A regular rectangular shape is the best.

▦ A kitchen is luckier placed on the right of the main door. When it is placed on the left or directly in line with the main door, there tend to be many quarrels between husband and wife.

should take care to be very precise when investigating the compass direction and location of your gas cooker, and move it somewhere else if it is in the northwest if this is at all possible.

This kitchen is badly arranged
in terms of feng shui and will prove
damaging to the family's prosperity
and well-being.

PLACEMENT OF THE COOKER

Reputations can be substantially hurt
when there are problems with the
cooker location. Feng shui strenuously
warns successful men and women always
to take good care of their cookers (or rice
cookers if their staple food is rice). This
is because fame and reputation luck
are very vulnerable if the cooker is
placed in the wrong position or facing
the wrong direction.

ORIENTATION OF THE COOKER

The cooker should have its source of
energy coming from the direction that
represents your personal success direction.
If this is not possible, try to tap one of the
other three directions that belong to your
group of directions. Try at all costs to avoid
having the cooker get its energy from any
one of your four inauspicious directions,
as this could lead to lawsuits, scandals,
and a fall from grace.

This kitchen has the furniture and equipment arranged so that the chi can flow through freely, and there are no clashing elements.

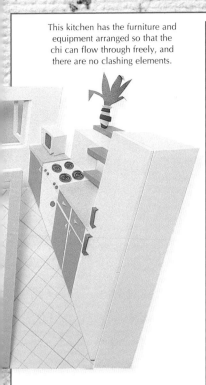

SIMPLE GUIDELINES

- ▨ The cooker should not face the main door.
- ▨ The cooker should not face the toilet or bathroom door.
- ▨ The cooker should not face the master bedroom door.
- ▨ The cooker should not be located directly under a beam.
- ▨ The cooker should not directly face a staircase.
- ▨ The cooker should not be in the northwest of the kitchen.
- ▨ The cooker should never be placed awkwardly or in a corner.
- ▨ The cooker should not be sandwiched between two sinks or taps. This symbolizes tears within the family, caused by a severe misfortune or loss.

TAKE CARE

The energies created by the cooker are extremely strong. It is thus advisable to be careful that these energies do not hurt the important areas of the home. In feng shui, however, it is not always possible to get everything right. So where a choice has to be made between different options, always choose to protect the main door.

THE TIME DIMENSION

USING FLYING STAR FENG SHUI

This type of feng shui addresses the changes of feng shui over time. This popular method is widely used in Hong Kong, Malaysia, and Singapore. Flying star feng shui complements the space dimension of other feng shui methods, adding the vital dynamics of the time factor. This is a very advanced method and it is not really necessary for amateur practitioners to get too involved in the technical details of its computations. However, it is useful to have a reference table to enable you to investigate the impact of flying star on your own feng shui, particularly since this method is excellent for warning against the flying stars that bring serious bad luck. Being forewarned is often a great way of avoiding bad luck.

WHAT ARE THE FLYING STARS?

The stars refer to the numbers one to nine placed around a nine-sector grid, known as the Lo Shu magic square. The numbers around the grid fly – they change over time. The way they do this forms the crux of this method of feng shui.

Every day, month, and year, and every 20-year period has its own arrangement of numbers around the square. Every number has its own meanings and tells the feng shui expert who knows how to interpret the numbers a great many things. For the purpose of being forewarned, it is sufficient to monitor the period and year stars.

SOUTH

4	9	2
3	5	7
8	1	6

THE PERIOD OF SEVEN

We are currently living through the period of seven, which started in 1984 and does not end until the year 2003. This means that during this period, the number seven is deemed to be very lucky. The Lo Shu square for this period is shown here. Through an interpretation of the numbers, it describes the fortunate and less fortunate sectors up to the year 2003.

SOUTH

6	2	4
5	7	9
1	3	8

The original nine-sector Lo Shu square has the number five in the center. The numbers have been arranged so that the sum of any three numbers, taken vertically, horizontally or diagonally, is 15. In flying star feng shui, the numbers move from grid to grid and they are then interpreted according to which of them is in which square. Each of the eight sectors on the outside of the square represents a corner of the home. For analysis, the center is the ninth sector. South is placed at the top according to tradition, for presentation purposes only. Use a compass to identify the actual corners of your home.

During the period of seven, the bad-luck star number five is located in the east. This is interpreted to mean that if the main door of your home is located in the east, you should be very careful during this 20-year period. It also means that those sleeping in bedrooms located in the east should also be extra careful against being stabbed in the back.

The analysis will be more accurate when investigation is also conducted on the star numerals during the month and the year in question. When two or all three star numerals are fives in the same sector, loss due to extreme bad luck is certain during that month and year for anyone whose bedroom is in the sector where the fives occur together! When you become aware of the time when you need to be extra careful, one way of countering the bad luck is to travel away from home. Go for a vacation during that period, thereby avoiding the bad luck.

Year	Star numeral 2 is in the	Star numeral 5 is in the
1997	Southeast	West
1998	Center	Northeast
1999	Northwest	South
2000	West	North
2001	Northeast	Southwest
2002	South	East
2003	North	Southeast
2004	Southwest	Center
2005	East	Northwest
2006	Southeast	West

Year	Month 1	Month 2	Month 3	Month 4	Month 5
1997	Southwest	East Northwest	Southeast West	Northeast	South Northwest
1998	Northeast	Northwest South	West North	Northeast Southwest	South East
1999	Northeast Southwest	South East	North Southeast	Southwest	East Northwest
2000	Southwest	East Northwest	Southeast West	Northeast	Northwest South
2001	Northeast	Northwest South	West North	Northeast Southwest	South East

ROOMS TO AVOID
DURING SPECIFIC PERIODS
The yearly reference table
(*based on the lunar year)

The table opposite shows where the star five and star two occur together. The star two combined with five makes it extra dangerous and brings illness.

THE MONTHLY REFERENCE TABLES.
(*based on the lunar months)

The table below indicates the dangerous sectors during each of the 12 lunar months over the next five years. These are the sectors where the star

Based on the reference table on the left, rooms in the south are prone to illness in 1999. In 2002 rooms in the south and east should be avoided, and in 2005 rooms in the east should be avoided.

numerals two and five are located during that month. In the years 1998 and 2001 there are 13 months, so one of the months has been doubled.

Match where the star numerals two and five fall during the months indicated with those of the annual star numerals and the 20-year period star numerals.

Where twos and fives occur together is when that sector becomes dangerous and anyone occupying a room in an afflicted sector would do well to leave it for that time. Be particularly careful when the star numerals two and five fall into the east sector. This is because this is the sector afflicted with the five in the 20-year period flying star. The danger months and the directions are marked. When there are two dots, it means that both the sectors indicated are dangerous.

Month 6	Month 7	Month 8	Month 9	Month 10	Month 11	Month 12
West North	Northeast Southwest	South East	North Southeast	Southwest	East Northwest	Southeast West
South East	North Southeast	Southwest	East Northwest	Southeast West	Northeast	Northwest South
Southeast West	Northeast	Northwest South	West North	Northeast Southwest	South East	North Southeast
West North	Northeast Southwest	South East	North Southeast	Southwest	East Northwest	Southeast West
North Southeast	Southwest	East Northwest	Southeast West	Northeast	Northwest South	West North

INDEX

FURTHER READING

Kwok, Man-Ho and O'Brien, Joanne,
The Elements of Feng Shui,
ELEMENT BOOKS, SHAFTESBURY, 1991

Lo, Raymond *Feng Shui: The Pillars of
Destiny (Understanding Your Fate and
Fortune),* TIMES EDITIONS, SINGAPORE, 1995

Skinner, Stephen, *Living Earth Manual
of Feng Shui: Chinese Geomancy,*
PENGUIN, 1989

Too, Lillian, *Basic Feng Shui,*
KONSEP BOOKS, KUALA LUMPUR, 1997

Too, Lillian, *The Complete Illustrated
Guide to Feng Shui,* ELEMENT BOOKS,
SHAFTESBURY, 1996

Too, Lillian, *Chinese Astrology for
Romance and Relationships,*
KONSEP BOOKS, KUALA LUMPUR, 1996

Too, Lillian *Chinese Numerology
in Feng Shui,* KONSEP BOOKS,
KUALA LUMPUR, 1994

Too, Lillian, *Dragon Magic,*
KONSEP BOOKS, KUALA LUMPUR, 1996

Too, Lillian *Feng Shui,* KONSEP BOOKS,
KUALA LUMPUR, 1993

Too, Lillian *Practical Applications for
Feng Shui,* KONSEP BOOKS,
KUALA LUMPUR, 1994

Too, Lillian *Water Feng Shui for Wealth,*
KONSEP BOOKS, KUALA LUMPUR, 1995

Walters, Derek *Feng Shui Handbook:
A Practical Guide to Chinese Geomancy
and Environmental Harmony,*
AQUARIAN PRESS, 1991

USEFUL ADDRESSES

Feng Shui Design Studio
PO Box 705, Glebe, Sydney, NSW 2037,
Australia, Tel: 61 2 315 8258

Feng Shui Society of Australia
PO Box 1565, Rozelle, Sydney
NSW 2039, Australia

The Geomancer
The Feng Shui Store
PO Box 250, Woking, Surrey GU21 1YJ
Tel: 44 1483 839898
Fax: 44 1483 488998

Feng Shui Association
31 Woburn Place, Brighton BN1 9GA,
Tel/Fax: 44 1273 693844

Feng Shui Network International
PO Box 2133, London W1A 1RL,
Tel: 44 171 935 8935,
Fax: 44 171 935 9295

The School of Feng Shui
34 Banbury Road, Ettington,
Stratford-upon-Avon, Warwickshire
CV37 7SU. Tel/Fax: 44 1789 740116

The Feng Shui Institute of America
PO Box 488, Wabasso, FL 32970,
Tel: 1 407 589 9900 Fax: 1 407 589 1611

Feng Shui Warehouse
PO Box 3005, San Diego, CA 92163,
Tel: 1 800 399 1599 Fax: 1 800 997 9831

"I want to say special words of thanks to my Editor, **Caro Ness** who has done an absolutely brilliant job tightening my manuscripts yet staying so true to the essence of each of the subjects of the nine books.

I must also acknowledge the vision of **Julia McCutchen** whose belief in this series was what brought out the best in me. Thank you both."

**Other titles in the
Feng Shui Fundamentals
series are:**

Careers
Children
Education
Eight Easy Lessons
Health
Love
Networking
Wealth